WHITBY AT WORK

PAUL CHRYSTAL

AMBERLEY

ACKNOWLEDGEMENTS

Thanks to Whitby & Scarborough Harbours, Scarborough Borough Council for allowing access to the Fish Quay, to Colin Hinson for permission to quote from his Yorkshire history pages at www.genuki.org.uk/big/eng/YKS/, to Roger Pickles at the Whitby Museum for permission to reproduce images from the fabulous Doran Collection (ww.whitbymuseum. org.uk/whats-here/collections/hidden-collections/photographs/) and to Whitby Online (www.whitbyonline.co.uk) for allowing me to use images from their site – and to the copyright holders W. D. Varney ARPS and Christine & Janine (née Watson). My gratitude too to Sally Atkinson at Parkol Marine Engineering for permission to use the two images from their website and to Sid Weatherill who took the pictures. Thanks to the following Whitby businesses for allowing me to take photographs on their premises: the Whitby Jet Heritage Centre, Fortunes, Sandgate Seafoods Ltd, and Natural Wonders.

Front cover: Building ships at Parkol. (Courtesy of Parkol Marine and Sid Weatherill. © Sid Weatherill)

First published 2019

Amberley Publishing
The Hill, Stroud
Gloucestershire, GL5 4EP

www.amberley-books.com

Copyright © Paul Chrystal, 2019

The right of Paul Chrystal to be identified as the Author of this work has been asserted in accordance with the Copyrights, Designs and Patents Act 1988.

ISBN 978 1 4456 8515 1 (print)
ISBN 978 1 4456 8516 8 (ebook)

British Library Cataloguing in Publication Data.
A catalogue record for this book is available from the British Library.

Origination by Amberley Publishing.
Printed in the UK.

CONTENTS

INTRODUCTION

Think of Whitby and you may think first of fish (and chips). Indeed, while fish and fishing has served the town well for hundreds of years, tourism is now the key industry, providing work for thousands of local people, all cultivating the huge interest in Whitby's Gothic culture, jet and the abbey, all of which attract many thousands of visitors every year. Many of these depend on the hospitality the town has to offer in terms of numerous holiday cottages, hotels, cafés, restaurants and pubs, and avail themselves of the beaches, boat trips and museums.

This book charts and explores the work, commerce and industry that has characterised Whitby down the years, and which shapes the town today in the early twenty-first century. Whitby plays a major role in the religious and ecclesiastical history of the United Kingdom, not least with the grand and imposing ruins of Whitby Abbey, which stand atop the magnificent towering East Cliff. The focus on fishing began in the reign of Elizabeth I (r. 1558–1603). By the beginning of the seventeenth century alum (which up until now was all imported) had become

The Magpie Café, a posh fish and chip shop and seafood restaurant that is beloved by Rick Stein and many others.

Above and below: Whitby to the west and Whitby to the east.

prominent and mining here helped England become self-sufficient when foreign imports were banned. The alum helped the port to grow through distribution, and through the importation of coal down from the Durham coalfield to process it.

With its fame for fish and fishing, its religious heritage and the obsession with the Gothic it is easy to forget that Whitby is also a vibrant market town with a twice weekly market and a fine market square dating from 1640 to accommodate it. Additionally, the immediate hinterland supports a productive agricultural industry from which much of the produce finds its way into Whitby market. The market had moved from Golden Lion Bank to take advantage of the increased footfall on the east side courtesy of Sir Hugh Cholmley's new 1767 drawbridge replacing the 1609 bridge.

Above: The 1767 bridge.

Left: It's not all fish in Whitby. Farming in the Whitby hinterland, a Frank Meadow Sutcliffe classic entitled *Dinner Time*, from *Sun Artists: A Serial of Artistic Photography* (1889).

Shipbuilding came on stream, and was at its peak in 1790–91 when Whitby built 11,754 tons of shipping, making it the third largest shipbuilder in England, after London and Newcastle. Import taxes financed the town's twin piers, improving the harbour and opening the town up to more trade.

The year 1753 saw the first whaling ship set sail to Greenland, making Whitby a major whaling port by 1795 with all the benefits of trading in whale oil and whale bone, which was used for lighting and for 'stays' in the corsetry trade.

Above: The fishing fleet and fish quay.

Right: The famous whalebone jaws dominating the town, an icon for Whitby's whaling heritage.

The Georgian period saw the start of tourism when Whitby developed as a spa town. This was boosted in 1839 when the Whitby and Pickering Railway connected Whitby to Pickering and then to York. The Larpool Viaduct and the construction of the A171 road bridge over the River Esk increased and improved communications further.

In the early twentieth century the fishing fleet came to prominence and even as recently as 1972 the number of boats using the port was 291, up from sixty-four in 1964. Timber, paper and chemicals were imported, and steel, furnace bricks and doors were exported.

Today, tourism – not least the magnetic draw of all things Gothic – is vitally important. For the twenty-first-century local economy it is hoped that the proposed offshore Dogger Bank Wind Farm will put the wind back in Whitby's economic and industrial sails. Work is underway on Sirius Minerals' huge potash mine near Whitby, which will be linked to a processing facility at Wilton in Redcar on Teesside by a 23-mile underground tunnel.

The Whitby Marina project, jointly funded by Scarborough Borough Council, Yorkshire Forward and the European Regional Development Fund, was developed to add depth to and diversify the local economy. The sole remaining shipbuilding firm, Parkol Marine, is a family-run business founded in 1988.

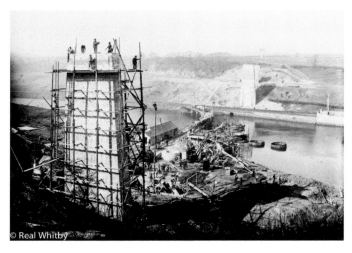

© Real Whitby

Building the road bridge over the River Esk in 1980, which cost £2 million.

Red Whitby roofs from the 199 steps in the twenty-first century.

GOD'S WORK

WHITBY ABBEY AND HILDA

God's hand, and his work, is unmissable and unmistakable in the Whitby landscape, thanks primarily to the dramatic ruins of Whitby Abbey, which are visible for many miles around by land and out at sea, and towers over the town below. Its mother house was Fountains Abbey in the diocese of York. Originally established in AD 657 as a Christian monastery, it was later to become a Benedictine abbey. This monastery was founded by the Anglo-Saxon

The sun goes down on Whitby Abbey, thanks largely to Henry VIII. (Photographer: Ackers72)

King of Northumbria Oswy (AD 612–670) and named Streoneshalh, the original name for Whitby. Whitby essentially owes its origin to the abbey: Oswy did a deal with God when he redeemed a vow that he had made before the AD 655 Battle of Leeds that if God would grant him victory over Penda, the pagan King of Mercia who had invaded his territory, he would build a monastery, and consecrate his daughter, Ethelfleda, then just one year old, to God's services through a life of celibacy. God heard the prayers of Oswy; Penda was slain with most of his nobles, and Oswy duly built the monastery of Streanshalh, for monks and nuns of the Benedictine order. He installed Hilda, abbess of Hartlepool Abbey and grand-niece of Edwin, the first Christian king of Northumbria, as founding abbess. The abbey and all its possessions were, however, confiscated by the crown during the Dissolution of the Monasteries under Henry VIII. However, Henry was not the only destructive force:

the rudest shock it received in modern times was from a storm of wind in the night of the 2nd of December, 1763, when the whole western wing was overturned and thrown down to the very foundations, though supported by at least twenty strong Gothic pillars and arches, nothing being left standing thereon but the north wall of the cloisters and a part of the wall at the west end… Whitby abbey stands on an eminence eighty yards at least above the sea, but if the situation is bleak the prospect is commanding, and presents a view of the town and port of Whitby, with the frowning heights of the black moors rising in the horizon in front, while in the rear is the vast expanse of the ocean, and the *tout ensemble* is truly magnificent. (www.genuki.org.uk/big/eng/YKS/NRY/Whitby/WhitbyHistory)

Apart from the extensive physical work and labour expended on the construction of the abbey over some 200 years in which scores of masons and other artisans toiled, the abbey symbolises the significant religious work that was going on in Whitby.

Hilda of Whitby (c. 614–680) is a Christian saint, one of the patron saints of learning and culture, and the founding abbess of the monastery at Whitby. She was an influential figure in the conversion of the Anglo-Saxons to Christianity, and her first convent was on the north bank of the River Wear where she learned all about Celtic monasticism, which Bishop Aidan introduced from Iona. Aidan appointed Hilda as the second abbess of Hartlepool Abbey. In 657 Hilda became the founding abbess of Whitby Abbey where she remained until her death in 680. The monastery, though dedicated to St Peter, is usually called St Hilda's after her.

According to Bede, in his 'Historia ecclesiastica gentis Anglorum', 'Ecclesiastical History of the English People', she was a prominent and energetic administrator and teacher, and much sought after as a wise counsel for visiting kings and princes. She nurtured the talented Caedmon, a herdsman at the monastery, who was inspired in a dream to sing verses in praise of God. Bede leaves us with this eulogy of Hilda: 'All who knew her called her mother because of her outstanding devotion and grace … she taught the observance of righteousness, mercy, purity and other virtues, but especially of peace and charity.' The work that Hilda did in Whitby consolidated the town's position at the forefront of religious politics and power throughout and after her reign.

Hilda was succeeded as abbess by Eanflæd, widow of King Oswiu, and their daughter, Ælfflæd. The abbey was sacked by the Danes in 867 under Ivar and Ubba and languished desolate and derelict for more than 200 years. After the Norman Conquest monks from Evesham under a monk called Reinfrid rebuilt the abbey in the Gothic style as a Benedictine house for men, and so it remained until the Dissolution of the Monasteries by Henry VIII in 1539.

Detail from *St. Hilda at Hartlepool* by James Clark James' oil painting. (Hartlepool Art Gallery, People's Choice, 12 August–17 September 2006. Author: Yaffa)

Historia ecclesiastica gentis Anglorum Beda Petersburgiensis, fol. 3v dated AD 746.

CAEDMON

Caedmon (fl. *c.* AD 657–684) is the earliest English poet whose name is known to us. His work attests to the importance of Whitby as a major Christian centre. Bede records that one night Caedmon went to bed ignorant of 'the art of song' but learned to compose during a dream. Caedmon's only known extant work is 'Caedmon's Hymn', the nine-line alliterative vernacular eulogistic poem in honour of God, *principium creaturarum*, 'the beginning of created things'. According to Bede, though, Caedmon produced a large number of splendid vernacular poetic texts on a variety of Christian topics. His list of Caedmon's oeuvre includes accounts of creation, translations from the Old and New Testaments, and songs about the 'terrors of future judgment, horrors of hell, … joys of the heavenly kingdom, … and divine mercies and judgments'. From then on he became a zealous monk and a talented and inspirational Christian poet. Bede wrote:

> [t]here was in the Monastery of this Abbess a certain brother particularly remarkable for the Grace of God, who was wont to make religious verses, so that whatever was interpreted to him out of scripture, he soon after put the same into poetical expressions of much sweetness and humility in Old English, which was his native language. By his verse the minds of many were often excited to despise the world, and to aspire to heaven.

The poet Laureate Alfred Austin unveiled Caedmon's Cross in 1898.

Caedmon's Cross.

THE SYNOD OF WHITBY

It is a mark of Whitby's importance in English ecclesiastical history, and of the religious work that was going on there, that the pivotal Synod of Whitby was held in the town in AD 664. This was a highly influential theological conference convened to determine conclusively the way ahead for the Christian church in England.

Essentially, King Oswiu of Northumbria decreed that his kingdom would calculate the date of Easter and observe the monastic tonsure according to the customs of Rome, rather than the customs practised by Irish monks at Iona and affiliated institutions. Christianity in Britain during the seventh century was a binary affair with different liturgical traditions, one the Ionan, the other the Roman tradition. In Northumbria, these two traditions coexisted, and each had been encouraged by different royal houses: first Edwin of Northumbria who had been converted to Christianity by missionaries sent from Rome by Pope Gregory the Great and then Oswald of Northumbria who had had learned his Christianity from the monks of Iona, and had encouraged Ionan missionaries to further the Christianisation of Northumbria, especially Bishop Aidan.

One sticking point was the calculation of Easter but finally the Synod established Roman practice as the norm in Northumbria. It settled the issue of Easter calculation and established the proper monastic tonsure, another highly contentious issue that was also decided in favour of the Roman way.

On a less godly, more satanic level the ruinous abbey gained celebrity status with the publication of Bram Stoker's 1897 novel *Dracula*, who leapt ashore as a large dog-like beast and proceeded to bound up the 199 steps that lead to the ruins. Whitby is today a world-famous Mecca for all things Gothic.

A scribe, thought to be Bede, who described the events of the Synod of Whitby in the early eighth century, depicted in a twelfth-century manuscript.

Above left, above right and left: The destruction wreaked by an unhindered German Navy: Abbey Lodge, West Hill School, Springfield Road, and the Coastguard Station.

The fateful morning of 16 December 1914 saw more hell unleashed when Whitby Abbey was shelled by the German battlecruisers *Von der Tann* and *Derfflinger* during a raid which also bombarded Scarborough and Hartlepool, with significant loss of life and widespread destruction. In Hartlepool the shelling killed sixty-three civilians and nine soldiers, and fifty-six civilians died in West Hartlepool. Four hundred or so civilians were injured and much housing stock was damaged or destroyed. In Scarborough and Whitby eighteen and three people were killed respectively. As they passed Whitby the cruisers fired fifty rounds at the signal station, town and abbey. The Royal Navy was nowhere to be seen – Churchill, the First Lord of the Admiralty, was having a bath at the time.

ST MARY'S CHURCH AND THE 199 STEPS

At the top of the 199 steps leading is Caedmon's Cross and the delightful St Mary's, an Anglican parish church founded around 1110, although its interior is largely late eighteenth century. It still has its eighteenth-century box pews, some of which are inscribed 'For Strangers Only'. North of the chancel arch is a Jacobean pew.

Caedmon's Cross today with St Mary's tower.

This is how Bram Stoker described St Mary's Church graveyard as the setting for a scene in his *Dracula*:

> For a moment or two I could see nothing, as the shadow of a cloud obscured St. Mary's Church. Then as the cloud passed I could see the ruins of the Abbey coming into view; and as the edge of a narrow band of light as sharp as a sword-cut moved along, the church and churchyard became gradually visible... It seemed to me as though something dark stood behind the seat where the white figure shone, and bent over it. What it was, whether man or beast, I could not tell.

The steps were actually originally made of wood until 1774 when they were replaced with Sneaton Stone. When St Mary's was still taking burials, many people expressed a preference that they be carried up the steps to be buried. Wooden planks were built at intervals to place the coffin on to give the pall bearers a rest, and they now serve as benches from which to admire the stunning views.

Caedmon's Cross looking out to West Cliff soon after 1898.

St Mary's graveyard.

ST. MARY'S PARISH CHURCH, WHITBY   1784

Above and below: Old and current views inside the beautiful St Mary's.

FISHING AND FISH

Whitby has always been a fishing port and fish has always been important to the town, and an inextricable part of its charm, economy and tourism.

Whitby fishermen are mentioned from the twelfth century. In 1635 one of our earliest records shows that the owners of the liberty of Whitby governed the port and town where twenty-four burgesses were given the privilege of buying and selling goods 'brought in by sea'.

It wasn't just fish here. The Whitby Brewing Company was also on the staith. Target Ales was one of their brews as available in the Elsinore Hotel at the end of Flowergate in the 1920s.

The Swing Bridge, built in 1908, separates the upper and lower harbours. Endeavour Wharf was completed in 1964. The Fish Quay, constructed in 1957, is 214 metres long.

Today, inshore fishing, particularly for shell and line fish, is active along the coast where lobsters and brown and velvet crabs are caught in abundance. From May to August, salmon from the Esk is netted off the harbour entrance. Herring has given way to cod, haddock,

Sandgate Seafoods' fish and shellfish shop with the jaws of a tiger shark and a mako shark.

Fortune's Smokehouse and Shop are the kipper specialist in Henrietta Street. The business was established in 1872 by William Fortune and is still in the family.

Kippers smoking in the smokehouse.

Taking the herrings to the smokehouse.

ling and other fish caught within 12 miles of the coast. Fish market auctions, though now infrequent, take place in the modern refrigerated Whitby Fish Market, which caters mainly for crab and lobsters.

Recent additions to the harbour facilities include a chilled bait store, built in 2005, on the fish market and a shellfish holding facility built in 2008.

The famous Magpie Café has always been connected with fishing and the shipping industry. It was built in 1750 as a merchant's house and at one time was owned by a member of the Scoresby whaling family. It has also housed the pilotage where the pilots would wait for orders to bring vessels into the harbour. The building later became Harrowing's shipping office.

A definite indicator of how dedicated the town is to its fishing heritage and its desire to project this into the future is the existence of the Whitby & District Fish Industry Training School, which was set up to provide education and training and promote the profile of the industry in the vicinity.

Fortune's in earlier days. (With kind permission of Roger Pickles, Joint Curator of Photographs, Whitby Museum and the Whitby Literary and Philosophical Society)

A Frank Sutcliffe image showing a sweep off to a call.

The quay in the 1960s.

Scottish herring girls on the Fish Quay on Pier Road. The herring shoals moved south down the Yorkshire coast in July and August, and the Scottish boats followed them, with their own girls to expertly gut the herrings and pack them with salt into barrels for trade at home and abroad.

Above and left: Whitby women preparing and selling Whitby fish.

'Confidences': Whitby fish girls. (A Frank Meadow Sutcliffe photograph)

Girls skaning mussels. The commercial fishing fleet at Whitby Harbour, though much depleted, ranges from large white fish trawlers to smaller day-fishing shellfish vessels.

Left: 'Fetching In the Lines'. The girl is Lizzie Alice Hawksfield, Next to her is her basket of mussels, used as bait. Skaning involved removing mussels from the shells, and mucking was cleaning lines and hooks of old bait. (A Frank Meadow Sutcliffe photograph)

Below: Two flither pickets with buckets full of limpets on the Scaur, the rock beach at Whitby's East Cliff. Flithers, or limpets, were used as bait. (A Frank Meadow Sutcliffe photograph)

Fish Jane, a celebrity fishwife. (Photographed by J. Stonehouse)

The fishing fleet bringing in the catch.

Produce at the Fish Quay in 2018.

Whitby fish market.

Whitby fishermen by the harbour rail.

Long-line fisherman with a boy. (A Frank Meadow Sutcliffe photograph)

WHALING

Commercial whaling in Britain began in the late sixteenth century, continued into the nineteenth century and then intermittently until the middle of the twentieth century when British companies exited the industry; whaling product imports were banned in 1973.

The year 1753 saw the first whaling ship set sail to Greenland when two ships formed the Whitby Whaling Company and set off from Whitby. These ships were crewed by forty to fifty hands, by local fishermen and more experienced Dutch whaling experts. By 1795 Whitby had become a major whaling port. Between 1753 and 1833 there were fifty-five whaling ships operating out of the harbour, and by 1768 a Whitby ship, *Jenny*, was celebrated as one of the two most successful whaling ships in the whole of the British fleet. It is estimated that Whitby's whaling industry produced a harvest of over 25,000 seals, fifty-five polar bears and 2,761 whales.

The biggest bumper year was 1814 when eight ships caught 172 whales. The whaler the *Resolution's* catch yielded 42 tons of whale fins or whale bone and 1,390 tons of oil, which had manifold uses including a cleaning agent for wool before it was spun and as lubricants for factory machinery. Urbanisation increased the demand for lamp fuel and its use in street lighting. The building industry used whale oil as an ingredient in paint, varnish and putty. The carcases produced 42 tons of whale bone for 'stays' as used in the corsetry trade. In Whitby blubber was boiled to produce oil for use in lamps in four boiler houses on the harbourside. The Whitby Whale Oil and Gas Company became the Whitby Coal and Gas Company to reflect the expansion of gas lighting in Whitby. As the market for whale products fell, catches became too small to be economic and by 1831 only one whaling ship, the *Phoenix*, remained.

When the fleet returned to Whitby after a voyage, the ships mast indicated how successful the trip had been: if the fleet had been successful then whales' jaw bones would be fixed to the masts. This gave rise to Whitby's striking whale jaw archway, originally gifted to Whitby by Norwegian Thor Dhal and the artist Graham Leach in 1963 in recognition of the dangers faced by the whalers and as a tribute to Whitby's whaling heritage.

This deteriorating bone arch was replaced in 2002. The current whale bones were donated by Whitby's sister town of Anchorage, Alaska, which were found abandoned after a legal hunt on Alaska's northern coast.

Three men closely associated with Whitby's maritime heritage did sterling, ground-breaking work. They are Captain James Cook (1728–79), Captain William Scoresby Snr and Revd William Scoresby (1789–1857).

Captain James Cook

Explorer, navigator, cartographer, and Royal Navy captain, Cook created detailed maps of Newfoundland before making three voyages to the Pacific Ocean, during which he made the first European contact with the eastern coastline of Australia and the Hawaiian Islands, and the first circumnavigation of New Zealand. Cook was born in Marton near Middlesbrough. In 1745 he moved the 20 miles south to Staithes to be apprenticed as a shop boy to grocer and haberdasher William Sanderson. After eighteen months Cook moved on to Whitby to be introduced to friends of Sanderson's, John and Henry Walker, Quakers and prominent local shipowners in the coal trade. Their house in Grape Lane, euphemistically rebadged from Grope Lane, as in York, is now the Captain Cook Memorial Museum. Cook embarked on an apprenticeship in their small fleet taking coals from Newcastle down the coast. His first

Captain Cook and his
monument.

posting was aboard the collier *Freelove*. During this time Cook studied algebra, geometry,
trigonometry, navigation and astronomy.

HMS *Endeavour*, the ship commanded by Cook on his voyage to Australia and New Zealand,
was built in Whitby in 1764 by Tomas Fishburn as a coal carrier with the name *Earl of Pembroke*.
The Royal Navy bought her in 1768, refitted and renamed her.

Captain William Scoresby Snr and Revd William Scoresby

Captain William Scoresby Snr (1760–1829) was born in Cropton near Pickering, which is 20
miles south of Whitby, on a farmstead. He became a successful whaler and Arctic explorer
whose numerous discoveries, research and accomplishments included the invention of the
crow's nest to provide shelter and safety for the navigator at the top of the main mast. The
crow's nest is a canvas covered frame with a hatch underneath for the lookout to climb
through and then stand at the top of the tallest mast with the telescope to his eye, scanning
the seas for whales.

When he was around nineteen, William Snr apprenticed himself to a Whitby shipowner, the
Quaker John Chapman. He served on the ship *Jane* operating in the Baltic trade. During the
winters he studied navigation.

His son, Revd William Scoresby (1789–1857), made his first sea trip with his father aged
eleven and at the age of seventeen he joined his father on board the whaling ship *Resolution* as
his father's chief officer. On his many Arctic voyages he began studying meteorology and the
natural history of the polar regions. In 1811, Scoresby assumed command of the *Resolution*
and that same year he married the daughter of a Whitby shipbroker. He was also in the habit
of making friends with polar bears. He experimented extensively in magnetism to discover
the effects of iron on compasses, which were growing less reliable as the amount of metal in
ships increased. He was thus able to create a more reliable compass needle. He mapped out
the east coast of Greenland in 1822 and studied the wildlife of this region, adding substantially
to our knowledge of navigation, polar flora and fauna and polar cartography. In 1856 he
travelled to Australia on the SS *Royal Charter* to measure changes in the angle of dip on either
side of the equator.

In 1813, he took command of a new ship built in Whitby called the *Esk*. The maiden voyage on the *Esk* was a successful one, both scientifically and commercially. Scoresby proved that the temperature of the sea is warmer below than on the surface. In 1820 he published the landmark *An Account of the Artic Regions*, the first ever scientific account of the region.

In 1826 he preached at St Mary's to mark the loss of two whaling ships that had sailed from the port. The *Lively* was lost with all hands in an Arctic storm and the *Esk* sank at Marske, less than 30 miles up the coast from Whitby. Sixty-five men were lost to the sea, twenty were from Shetlands and the remainder coming from Whitby. It was this loss that coincided with the end of Whitby's whaling industry.

The Scoresby Chair is in St Mary's Church, a beautifully carved teak chair salvaged from the wreck of the *Royal Charter*, the ship in which the Revd W. Scoresby Jnr sailed in his quest to improve the effectiveness of the compass.

The reconstructed *Endurance* in the Captain Cook Museum.

Painting of the *Earl of Pembroke*, later HMS *Endeavour*, leaving Whitby Harbour in 1768, by Thomas Luny (1759–1837). Dated to *c.* 1790. (Source/ Photographer www. nla.gov.au/nla.pic-an2280897)

Above: Views of the South Seas, one of a set of four (No. 3). View of Charlotte Sound in New Zealand (sic, actually a view in Matavai Bay, Tahiti). These hand-coloured aquatints were published by F. Jukes in 1787–88. The set of four aquatints relates to Cook's third voyage. The watercolours from which these prints were engraved were painted by James Cleveley, a carpenter on HMS *Resolution.* The original sketches were repainted by James's brother, John, and turned into aquatints by John Martyn.

Right: The Scoresby Chair.

EXTRACTING ALUM AND TAKING THE URINE

By a remarkable twist of fate at the end of the sixteenth century Sir Thomas Chaloner from Guisborough visited alum works at Puteoli and Tolfa in Italy under the control of the Pope, Clement VIII. Here he noticed that the rock being processed was similar to that which lay under his estate in Belham Bank, near Guisborough. Also he recognised that that the discolouration of leaves on trees near the Pope's alum works resembled those near his own home. Chaloner's mission was made all the more urgent since the alum supply to Britain was compromised during the Renaissance. The Pope's alum-making technique was to roast the rock for a year, soak it in potassium and stale urine and then warm the mixture back up until enough liquid had evaporated to allow a fresh chicken's egg to float to the surface.

Alum production was a disgusting and highly polluting process. It involved building 100 foot pyramids of burning shale and keeping them going night and day for months on end. It necessitated a whole production line of quarrying, extraction, steeping, boiling, evaporating, crystallisation, milling and bagging up for export. Quarrying alone devastated the surrounding cliffs, along with the razing of the forests for charcoal and the poisoning of the land with sulphuric acid and ash. The north-east's relative remoteness contributed to systemised, round-the-clock production, exploitation of an impoverished workforce and widespread environmental damage. Stephen Chance asked in *The Guardian* on 20 November 2013: 'Was alum the first example of the north-east's "dirty" industries?'

At that time alum had important medicinal uses, and it was vital in curing leather to render hide supple and workable, and for fixing dyed cloths. Italy and Spain enjoyed monopolies on its production and sale, two countries that unfortunately happened to be in conflict with England at the time. So a canny Chaloner discretely brought specialist workmen out of Italy to help develop the industry back home in Yorkshire. In 1607 a company was set up to exploit this find. New sources were discovered near Whitby and a patent was obtained. The result was that alum was produced near Sandsend Ness, which is 3 miles from Whitby. The Pope of course was incandescent and brought down the wrath of God on Chaloner, calling on all holy institutions from 'God Almighty, the Father, Son and Holy Ghost' to rain curses on all those who spirited alum expertise away from Italy.

The Pope had been exporting alum to England at £52 a ton, but the new supply for the British market was a mere £11 per ton. However, for the next twenty-five years the company struggled to produce adequate supplies for the home market and thus justify a ban on imports. It suffered heavy financial losses. It was not until 1635 that output reached the stipulated 1,800 tons per annum and not until 1648 that the alum monopoly was abolished and an import ban could be imposed. As a result new alum works sprang up all along the Yorkshire coast at suitable outcrops of the Upper Lias shale, not least at Sandsend and nearby Ravenscar. At Loftus Alum Quarries the cliff profile has been drastically changed by extraction and huge shale tips remain. Remains of stone breakwaters and berths are visible at Saltwick Bay.

Once the industry was running productively enough imports were banned and England eventually became self-sufficient. Whitby owes much of its growth as a port to the alum trade and by importing huge supplies of coal from the Durham coalfield to process it.

Alum was, as noted, used as a mordant to fix colour into woollen cloths. In around 1595, during the reign of Elizabeth I, the Tudor textile industry accounted for about 80 per cent of Britain's exports, so alum was very important and a crucial element in the nation's balance of payments, productivity and export success.

Many tons of shale and rock were quarried from the local cliffs. To create the alum crystal from this shale, it took 10 tons of coal to fire the burning process for every 1 ton of alum. As with the papal method, after several months of slow burning, the stacks, or 'clasps', of heated shale were broken open to reveal the white mineral within: this was the alum ready for rendering. These former stacks are still visible in the Sandsend works and at Ravenscar. A winding house, which once housed the winching machine, survives at Ravenscar, and the iron fittings and spindle wheels are still intact. It was used to haul coal deliveries up the cliff, and to load the finished alum product on to ships in the dock below. At the peak of alum production the industry required 200 tons of urine every year, equivalent to the output of 1,000 people.

The consequent demand in and around Whitby for urine was insatiable – literally. From London to Newcastle buckets were placed on street corners and men were encouraged to urinate into them. A man with a horse and cart would came round and decant the buckets into barrels. The barrels were shipped to Whitby where they were stored with all their rancid odours on the Market Place. In the last two months of 1612 alone, Whitby's alum works consumed 29,000 gallons of urine – 16,000 of it 'country urine' and 13,000 'London urine'.

Remains of Peak alum works at Ravenscar.

The last alum works on the Yorkshire coast closed in 1871 in Kettleness and Boulby after it was discovered that the same mordant qualities could be obtained from coal and then by manufacturing synthetic alum in 1855, then subsequently by the creation of aniline dyes, which contained their own fixative.

Urine transportation has made a significant contribution to our national phraseology. Allegedly, sailors plying the urine trade were embarrassed by their cargo and when asked what they had in their barrels they replied 'beer and wine'. The scornful reply inevitably came: 'No way', retorted the scoffers, 'you're taking the piss.'

The alum industry was Britain's first chemical industry. Its ruinous quarries and works illustrate the early stages of the industry and the technological advances through the Industrial Revolution.

THE PORT AND SHIPBUILDING

Whitby can claim to be the oldest port in Yorkshire and may well have operated in Roman times. When religious activity blossomed and flourished in the town the port was developed to support the Christian community. Fishing was the main trade until the eighteenth century when shipbuilding and whaling took over on a grand scale. Rope making (Goodwill's Ropery) and sailcloth manufacturing were all carried out here. Sanders was the pre-eminent sailcloth makers, opened near Tate Hill Pier in 1756 and were suppliers of the sails for Cook's *Endeavour* and most of the whaling fleet. There was a dye works out on the Esk estuary. Trade with the Baltic States, Scandinavia and the Low Countries was substantial, particularly with timber imports. Brown's timber yard was at Dock End.

Whitehall Shipyard was out on the estuary, and were famous wooden shipbuilders around 1860. Hobkirk's owned the Fishburn slipway, the yard from which all three of Cook's ships were originally launched. Daniel Defoe perceptively remarked: 'an excellent harbour … they build very good ships for the coal trade, and many of them too, which makes the town very rich.'

The Whitby collier brig or 'cat' could carry 600 tons of coal and operated economically and efficiently in the north-east coast coal trade.

The revitalisation of the port in the twentieth century came about by something of an accident. A strike at Hull docks in 1955 led to an importer asking whether Whitby could handle half a dozen potato boats from Belgium. The six ships successfully unloaded their 2,500 tons of potatoes on Fish Quay in June 1955 and the rebirth of the old port was assured. The first outgoing cargo was 545 tons of lime from the Vale of Pickering, despatched to Perth on 11 July 1958.

Endeavour Wharf, near the railway station, was opened in 1964 and the number of vessels using the port in 1972 was 291, up from sixty-four in 1964. Timber, paper and chemicals are imported while exports include steel, furnace bricks and doors.

The port of Whitby is obviously strategically placed for shipping to Europe, especially to the Low Countries and Scandinavia. Vessels of up to 3,000 tons deadweight tonnage are received at the wharf, which can load or unload two ships simultaneously. As of 2004 54,000 square feet (5,000 square metres) of dock space is used to store all-weather cargo and there is a 17,000-square-foot (1,600-square metre) warehouse for weather-critical cargoes.

The harbour.

Cobles in the harbour.

In 1973 a shuttle of vehicles ran between Whitby and a Helmsley sawmill, moving 600 tons of tree trunks from the Black Forest, the accidental harvest from two severe European storms. Before a radio link was obtainable, shore-to-ship signalling was done by the harbour master flashing his car lights from the seafront. The work of the town's dredger the *Esk*, commissioned in 1936, enabled the 1,800 ton Russian ship *Spartak*, the largest vessel yet to use the port, to sail in with timber from the White Sea. She drew 16 feet with the high tide obligingly providing just 16 feet 2 inches.

SHIPBUILDING

The end of the eighteenth century was Whitby's heyday as a shipbuilding port. Making good use of local timber, in 1706 Whitby was the sixth most major port in Britain, building 130 ships that year. In 1790–91 Whitby built 11,754 tons of shipping, making it the third largest shipbuilder in England (after London and Newcastle). Along with this, taxes on imports entering the port paid for the improvement and extension of the town's twin piers, improving the harbour and opening the door to further increases in trade.

The harbour from
Church Street.

Building ships at
Parkol. (Courtesy of
Parkol Marine and
Sid Weatherill. © Sid
Weatherill)

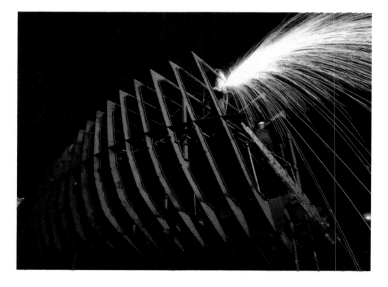

James Cook's three famous ships, HMS *Endeavour* (1764), HMS *Resolution* (1769) and HMS *Adventure* (1770), were all built at Thomas Fishburn's shipyard. The distinctive design of Whitby's flat bottomed 'cats' was perfectly suited for Cook's voyages of exploration in the South Seas when he had to land in unknown waters without harbours. The flat-bottomed design was also invaluable to the alum trade, for which ships needed to 'take the ground' safely. The *Resolution* was originally the North Sea collier *Marquis of Granby* before being bought by the Royal Navy in 1771 and repurposed. The *Adventure* started life as the cargo ship *Marquis of Rockingham* before being purchased and renamed by the Royal Navy. After being converted into a fire ship in 1780 the *Adventure* was sold back to Fishburn in 1780 as a cargo carrier between Britain and North America. She ended her days a wreck in the Saint Lawrence River in 1811.

The advent of iron ships in the late nineteenth century and the development of port facilities on the River Tees and at Hartlepool led to the decline of smaller Yorkshire harbours including Whitby. The *Monkshaven* launched in 1871 was the last wooden ship built at Whitby and a year later the harbour was silted up, so much so, in fact, that boys could play quoits on gravel in the middle.

The one remaining shipbuilding firm, Parkol Marine, is a family-run business on the east side of the River Esk. Founded in 1988, the boatyard has two work sheds (40 metres b 20 metres and 20 metres by 7 metres) with building births which can accommodate new builds up to 25 metres long and 8 metres beam. There is also a dry dock with a capacity of up to 5 metres draft, 42 metres long and 10.5 metres beam. The two original Whitby dry docks were in the California Beck and Spital Bridge areas.

PORT LIFE

Whitby, of course, like any other town, is defined by its industries, and its people are defined over time by the kind of work they did and do.

A bridge across the harbour was and is essential to the town's trade and industry. Whitby's swing bridge is first mentioned in 1351, a wooden structure that was replaced in 1610. The first drawbridge went up in 1766, allowing ships to go up and down the harbour. This was replaced in 1835 with a swivel bridge. The bridge that you cross today was built by the same company that built Blackpool Tower and was first opened in 1909.

Stern Realities, Frank Meadow Sutcliffe (1853–1941). (Los Angeles County Museum of Art, the Marjorie and Leonard Vernon Collection, gift of the Annenberg Foundation, acquired from Carol Vernon and Robert Turbin (M.2008.40.2223.22)

Arguments Yard. The peculiar name derives from a citing in mid-seventeenth-century deeds that would suggest that this yard belonged to a Thomas Argment and his family. The spelling remained the same for the yard until 1830, when it was changed to 'Arguments'. 'Argument' is an Anglicisation of the Flemish name 'Argoment'.

OPENING THE BRIDGE IN 1909

With the structure of the temporary bridge still visible, the crowds clamoured to try out the new swing bridge on its opening day, 24 July 1909. Costing £22,600, it was declared open by Mrs Gervase Beckett, the wife of the local MP. At the front of the crowd is an elderly lady who, as a little girl in 1835, crossed the old 1835 bridge on its opening day seventy-four years before. The aim of the new bridge was to allow Whitehalls Yard to build bigger boats, but it was too late – price and advanced technology competition from the progressive new yards in the Hartlepools damaged Whitby badly.

A high level bridge across the valley was suggested in 1866 by Francis Pickernell, engineer to Whitby Harbour, but nothing came of it.

Weekly markets were held on St Ann's Staith from 1445 to 1640. The staith dates from 1499, the present quay being 8 feet higher than a previous one, which had a row of houses supported on piles backing on to the harbour.

At the seaward end of the staith is Haggersgate. The Missions to Seamen building on the corner was built as a private house in 1817. The street gives into 'Coffee House End', where there was once the fish market and a building formerly used as a museum.

Opening the bridge in 1909.

Opening the bridge to allow the *Jolly Roger* to pass through in 2018.

St Ann's Staith from the drawbridge.

The drawbridge from St Ann's Staith.

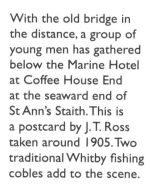

With the old bridge in the distance, a group of young men has gathered below the Marine Hotel at Coffee House End at the seaward end of St Ann's Staith. This is a postcard by J. T. Ross taken around 1905. Two traditional Whitby fishing cobles add to the scene.

A classic photo showing the buzz around the bridge and the Custom House Hotel.

The Dolphin Hotel, formerly known as Custom House Hotel, is on the right across the bridge. It was built on the site of old shops demolished in 1908. In the cellars of those shops it is said that there were shackles that had been used by the Royal Navy's press gang to hold their 'impressed' victims.

Tin Ghaut is a typical Whitby alleyway. 'Ghaut' is a Viking word meaning 'a narrow street leading to a river'. As an inn, the Britannia, was located at the end of the street, it became known as 'T'inn Ghaut'.

Next to Tin Ghaut was the vividly named Adler's Waste Ghaut, later renamed Virgin Pump Ghaut after a source of fresh running water. The pump was paid for by public subscription.

The lane also used to be known as Grape and before that Grope Lane because of its popularity with working girls and their clients. At the end of Grape Lane there is a cobbled piece of road, which is all that remains of the Potato Market known locally as Tatie Market.

Church Street is home to the Seamens' Hospital, founded in 1670, for distressed seamen and their dependents, providing houses paid for by a levy from ships passing through the port. The façade of the building was built in 1842 by Sir Gilbert Scott.

Over the road there used to be a passageway, used by smugglers, that ran from the harbourside underneath Church Street and came out in Elbow Yard. The first workhouses were founded here from 1727 to 1792. These old workhouses were later converted into tenements. There used to be a boatbuilding shop and workshop here.

The Market Square was built by Nathaniel Cholmley in 1788 and has been a focal point of the town since, acting as it does as a selling space for agricultural produce and wares of all sorts. The square itself replaced an older market place in 1640, when the old Tollbooth was demolished. The present hall, or Tollbooth, used to accommodate the country women selling their produce and, later, a pig market. The Courts Leet of the manor was held in the upper room, public whippings of thieves took place in the square, and the stocks were also here.

Lace stalls were also very popular, both here and on the Khyber Pass.

Above left, above right and below right: Three views of Tin Ghaut, an artist's and photographer's paradise but a resident's hell.

Ingathering in 1890 outside Whitby.

PRESS GANGS AND SMUGGLERS

Not all of Whitby's maritime activities were entirely voluntary, legitimate or legal. Like many other coastal settlements on the north east coast, Whitby made a name for itself as a centre of excellence for the smuggling trade and as a fertile hunting ground for the press gangs.

PRESS GANGS

The prospect of a life at sea under arms in the Royal Navy was less than attractive, so it is no surprise that every effort was made to dodge the king's shilling ('prest money'); indeed, enemy fire and shot apart, it is estimated that 50 per cent of the sailors on a given voyage would die of scurvy. And then there was the prospect of injurious or fatal naval combat, along with the additional annoying inconvenience that seamen's rights were not covered by the Magna Carta and 'failure to allow oneself to be pressed' was punishable by hanging.

Nor was your quaffing of a pint in the local quayside tavern always the relaxing and sociable experience it was intended to be. At any point the door might crash open and a mob of recruiting sergeants on a frenzied mission from His Majesty (under the name the Impress Service) would swarm in and manhandle you to the nearest vessel to impress you sufficiently to join the navy and see the world outside Whitby.

Impressment was used by the Royal Navy in wartime, beginning in 1664 and during the eighteenth and early nineteenth centuries, as a means of crewing warships (there was no conscription). Legal sanction for pressing can be traced back to the time of Edward I. People liable to impressment were 'eligible men of seafaring habits between the ages of 18 and 55 years'. Non-seamen were impressed as well, though not very often. The recruitment figures presented to Parliament for the years 1755–57 list 70,566 men, of whom 33,243 were volunteers (47 per cent), 16,953 pressed men (24 per cent), while another 20,370 were also listed as volunteers separately (29 per cent). In the eighteenth century, British desertion rates on naval ships averaged 25 per cent annually, with only a slight difference between volunteers and pressed men.

So undermanned had the navy become that in 1795, William Pitt brought two Quota Acts before Parliament. These commanded that each county had to provide a quota of men for enlistment in the Royal Navy according to its population and number of seaports. London had to produce 5,704 men, and Yorkshire, the largest county, were obliged to sign up 1,081. Whitby was an obvious and good source but compliance was not always what it should have been.

1780 caricature of a press gang.

'The Neglected Tar': a press gang seizing a seaman from his family (caricature), c. 1800. (Source/ Photographer www. collections.rmg. co.uk/collections/ objects/108923)

The crisis came to a head four years before the Napoleonic Wars (1799–1815). Officially they were restricted to seizing men who were experienced seamen, but in reality any man fitted the bill, and the age limits between eighteenth and fifty-five were likewise disregarded.

A famous recruitment incident took place in 1803 when the whaler *The Oak* sought refuge in Whitby's harbour from a ferocious storm. Whaleboat crews enjoyed reserved occupation status and were supposedly exempt, but the press gangs overlooked this; despite the screams and clashing of pots and pans from the quayside, the gang laid siege to the entire crew for enforced conscription. In the end, though, the locals caused such a commotion that they managed to spirit away the crew of *The Oak* through Whitby's snickelways and yards.

If you managed to elude the press gangs you could always indulge in a spot of smukkelling.

SMUGGLING

Show me a fisherman and I will show you a smuggler.

Anonymous eighteenth-century customs collector.

In Britain, wherever there was taxation of consumables there was smuggling, a word derived from the Scandinavian 'smugle' or 'smuggla' meaning 'to hide' or 'a hiding hole'. The first recorded use in English comes in an official document of 1661: 'A sort of lewd people called Smuckellors ... who make it their trade to steal and defraud His Majesty of His Revenue.'

Smuggling then was not a personal affront to the king, but was extremely crippling to the Exchequer, which was haemorrhaging revenue. Before this smuggling was referred to as 'frauds' and we first experience it in the late thirteenth century after the introduction of an eye-watering new tax, or custom, of 40 per cent on wool exports. Wool was our staple business then and was largely what made the country rich.

The Old Smuggler's Café of 1401 in Whitby's Brunswick Street unsurprisingly takes its name from the main use of the pub: it was previously known as 'The Old Ship Launch Inn' and it was well known that smugglers would use the pub to deliver their untaxed goods.

Just outside the carved wooden figurehead is believed to have once been part of a French smuggling vessel captured in 1830. Well before that the *Whitby Times* in 1790 reported:

Yesterday se'nnight the Fawn, smuggling luggar, with a thousand ankers of rum, brandy and geneva, to the amount of 6,000 gallons, was taken and sent into Whitby, by the Eagle cutter, Captain George Whitegead, in the service of the revenue of that port; with assistance of the Mermaid, Captain Carr. The Fawn is a fine clinch built vessel of 90 tonnes built at Flushing four months since, mounting six four pounders and six swivels. Her crew consisted of 22 men.

The added suggestion is that there was a secret tunnel that connects from the Old Smuggler's Café to the Station Hotel, which then led to the harbour, so that the contraband would arrive at the harbour and then transported via the tunnel to one of the two pubs.

Ye Old Ship Launch.

Whitby was always a challenge for the revenue men because the quays extended into the town centre and the network of ginnels and backyards facilitated concealment of goods and escape from the authorities.

Smuggling was never just man's work. The women of Whitby were welcomed into the trade as they were often less obtrusive and the revenue men seem to have naively assumed that women would never get involved in such a sordid and illegal business. In reality housewives would go to market wearing loose fitting clothes and return home with their clothes laden with a treasure trove of contraband booty. Mrs Gaskell, who lived in Whitby at the time, wrote in *Sylvia's Lovers*:

> There was a clever way in which certain Whitby women managed to bring in prohibited goods. In fact, when a woman did give her mind to smuggling, she was full of resources, and tricks, and impudence, and energy more so than any man.

Goods were transported inland on pony trails running from Robin Hood's Bay to Fylingdales Moor along a route known as the Fish Road or Salt Road. Many Robin Hood's Bay wives trudged these tracks carrying baskets of fish and smuggled silk around their waist. Reputedly they carried pig bladders full of gin under their petticoats.

One story relating to the impact locally on Whitby smuggling exemplifies both stupidity and arrogance in the protagonist. In 1803 Sir Charles Turner, 2nd Baronet of Kirkleatham Hall, near Redcar, and MP for Hull, had the temerity to proclaim in Whitby that he could acquire a bottle of claret at the ridiculously low price of 1s 6d and could get bottles for his friends at the same knockdown price. The good people of Whitby, not entirely without hypocrisy, condemned the man as a delinquent for his involvement in 'so infamous a transaction'. Indeed, embarrassment inflicted on the Whitby collector apart, Turner could have been prosecuted on at least two charges relating to the buying of and supplying of smuggled goods. Needless to say, he went scot-free whereas other less privileged people would have felt the full lash of the law. For example, in 1834 the eight-man crew of the fishing boat *La Saint Marie* were rumbled in Whitby with brandy and tobacco concealed on board. They were fined £100 each and sent to Northallerton Correction House as they were obviously unable to pay their fines.

Dodging the excise officers was never easy, but there was one man, a double agent so to speak, who managed it very well and his secret life went with him to the grave. Captain Harold Hutchinson, of the Guisborough-based Dragoons Guards, became the Whitby area customs officer. After a quayside riot the regiment had been posted to Whitby for three years for the very purpose of suppressing smuggling in the vicinity. However, Captain Hutchinson was not averse to helping himself to contraband that had been seized from smugglers, and then selling it on himself. He made a tidy sum from this and was able to build himself a luxury home in Skinner Street known as 'Harold Mansion', a home that he also used as a brothel to satisfy the needs of visiting seamen.

The government calculated that around a phenomenal £4 billion worth of revenue was evaporating with illegal imports of tobacco and alcohol every year. It is estimated that 80 per cent of all tea consumed in England was duty free and on a single smuggling trip 3,000 gallons of spirits could be imported. Gin, in fact, became so cheap that it was used for cleaning windows. Tea was the staple commodity for the smuggler for most of the eighteenth century. It is believed that most if not all the inhabitants of Saltburn, Staithes, Runswick Bay and Robin Hood's Bay were involved in the illicit trade, and Whitby too was not exempt. A labyrinthine network of caves, tunnels and concealed cupboards kept the contraband out of sight in all of these locations. The skippers of the ships and boats earned £250 a run, the sailors and overland porters £5 and the labourers and armed lookouts on the beach one guinea.

By 1701 things had deteriorated so much that the Customs Commissioners expanded their staff. John Becket was appointed to Staithes with a salary of £40 a year. John Brown was sent to Whitby as an additional land waiter to inspect cargoes at unlading, and Thomas Long as boatman to inspect the holds of ships. J. Sedgewick was made surveyor of Robin Hood's Bay and allowed to charge his horse to expenses. Later that century, the service was expanded again until each small harbour had its officer and boat crews, with riding officers and informers.

Records from the Whitby Customs House for 1728 reveal seizures of 27 gallons of brandy discovered at a house in Goathland on the Moors; 8 gallons of the same at a Skinningrove cottage; 12 gallons of brandy, 6 lbs each of coffee and tea and 8 more gallons of brandy and geneva buried in sand, caves, hedges and hiding holes in various parts of the Moors.

Whitby's greatest day came in January 1777 when Whitby Custom House could boast a haul of 650 gallons of gin, 79 lb of green tea, 200 lb of Bohea tea, 7 gallons of wine, 56 lbs of brown candy and the 44-ton boat in which some of these goods had been found. The gloss was wiped off a Robin Hood's Bay haul when the officer, who took 200 casks of brandy and geneva, 150 bags of tea, a chest of blunderbusses, and cartuche boxes for twenty men in an innkeeper's house during October 1779, had to confess that the booty had previously been snatched by smugglers in a raid on the Hartlepool Customs House.

In the next century, after spying a suspicious vessel near Runswick one August Monday, Lieutenant King's Whitby boat gave chase, and was eventually able to escort into harbour a 23-ton ship yielding 21 tubs of geneva, 7 tubs of brandy, 3 casks tobacco, 2 chests of tea and 28 casks of salt. The four prisoners were fined £100 each by the justices, but being unable to pay, they were incarcerated in York prison.

In 1773 two excise cutters, the *Mermaid* and the *Eagle*, were outgunned and chased out of Robin Hood's Bay by three smuggling vessels, a schooner and two shallops. In 1779 a pitched battle between smugglers and excise men took place in the dock over 200 casks of brandy and geneva and fifteen bags of tea.

LIFEBOATS AND LIGHTHOUSES

Keeping the seamen safe was and is a priority in any seaport, and Whitby was and is no exception. The harbour here is sheltered by the east and west piers, which both have a lighthouse and beacon. The west lighthouse, of 1831, is the taller of the two at 84 feet and the east lighthouse, built in 1855, is 54 feet high. On the west pier extension is a foghorn that blasts every thirty seconds in fog. New lights were fitted to both the lighthouse towers and the beacons in 2011. Whitby Lighthouse, operated by Trinity House, is located outside the town, to the south-east, on Ling Hill. Whitby Highlights, between Whitby and Hawsker, opened in 1858. The Low light was soon dispensed with and replaced by a fog horn – the Hawsker Bull bellowed its last in 1988. The Highlight was automated and de-manned in 1991.

The Whitby lifeboat story begins in 1802 when Francis Gibbons, the collector of customs at Whitby, took advantage of an offer from Lloyds of London who contributed £50 to the £160 cost of a Greathead lifeboat. 9 February 1861 was a busy, and tragic day for the lifeboat:

Whitby Lifeboat Station and RNLI Museum.

Time warp as this early sailing ship passes between the two lighthouses in 2018.

launched three times before 2.30 p.m. it saved all the crews from the *Gamma*, the *Clara* and the *Flora*; however, a fourth service to help the stricken, *Merchant*, saw twelve fatalities out of the thirteen men on board.

Despite frantic signalling by the coastguard, on 30 October 1914 the hospital ship HMHS *Rohilla* ran aground, hitting the rocks at 4.00 a.m. within sight of shore on Saltwick Nab, a reef around a mile east of Whitby during a full south-westerly gale and with the lighthouses unlit due to the war. The reef is around 400 yards offshore and the ship soon broke her back. The twenty lifeboats and forty boats were all smashed bar one. The *John Fielden*, the Whitby lifeboat, was launched first and took thirty-five people off in two trips at around 7:30 a.m. However, it suffered damage and took no further part in the rescue.

Of the 229 people on board, eighty-five lost their lives in the hospital ship disaster, most of whom are buried in the churchyard at Whitby. 146 of the 229 on board, including Captain Neilson and all five nurses, as well as *Titanic* survivor Mary Kezia Roberts, survived. One of the recommendations at the inquest was that Whitby has its own motor lifeboat.

Whitby's first motor lifeboat saved eighty-six lives in a service, which started in 1919 and ended in 1938, with 117 launches. There was another lifeboat station at Upgang, 1 mile north of Whitby, which operated for fifty-four years before closing in 1919. Contemporary with the *Margaret Harker Smith* at the Upgang Station was the *William Riley*.

The lifeboat just visible in the boathouse (on page 52) was the *Mary Ann Hepworth*. The *William Riley* boasts one of the RNLI's more unusual services – 1.5 miles inland at Ruswarp. Heavy rains in September 1931 caused flooding with waters over 8 feet deep in places. The village of Ruswarp was particularly badly hit, and the lifeboat was physically hauled to assist

The launch of the first RM *Ellist*. (With kind permission of Roger Pickles, Joint Curator of Photographs, Whitby Museum and the Whitby Literary and Philosophical Society)

Whitby Lifeboat Station under East Cliff in the early 1960s.

there from Whitby by seventy townsfolk. On arrival it was launched into the flood and saved five villagers from their cottages, including a ninety-year-old bedridden lady.

In January 1881 the brig *Visitor* foundered off Robin Hood's Bay during a blizzard. The crew took to their boat but were forced to remain outside the harbour. It was impossible to launch the Whitby lifeboat at Whitby and so eighteen horses and 200 or so men from Whitby and Robin Hood's Bay hauled the Whitby boat, the *Robert Whitworth*, the 6 miles from Whitby to the bay in snow drifts 7 feet deep in places. At the end of the two-hour trek the men lowered the lifeboat down the steep street towards the seas with ropes. The first launch had to be aborted – the oars were smashed by a wave. At this point John Skelton, a local man with local knowledge of the bay, waded in and swam towards the *Visitor*'s crew, plotting a safe route for the lifeboat, now with eighteen crew on board, to follow.

Rough seas and wrecks at Whitby.

WHITBY PIERS, ROUGH SEA.

This fascinating photograph shows the women of Runswick Bay launching the *Robert Patton: The Always Ready* in March 1940 to assist the *Buizerd* of Groningen. The six crew were saved. This was not the first time the women had helped: on 12th April 1901 most of the able-bodied men were at sea in their cobles when the lifeboat, the *Jonathan Stott*, was needed to offer assistance. Only boys and old men remained onshore at the time so the ladies decided that the men and boys would man the vessel and they would launch it. All the cobles returned to shore safely. (With kind permission of Roger Pickles, Joint Curator of Photographs, Whitby Museum and the Whitby Literary and Philosophical Society)

A harbourside view from around 1905 of the rowing lifeboat *John Fielden*. The volunteer crew is wearing their cork life jackets. J. T. Ross entitled this view 'Whitby's Brave Hearts' to encapsulate the courage crews had to have when rescuing survivors.

Whitby's valiant lifeboat crew of old.

The Lifeboat Museum.

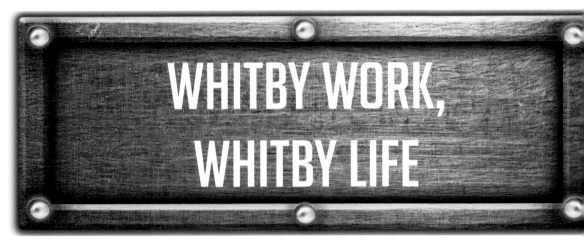

WHITBY WORK, WHITBY LIFE

There was a windmill, the Union Mill, in Union Place. Unusually it had five sails. Goodwill's Ropery was nearby on the Ropery. The original ropery here dates from 1721, and was 440 yards long. There was another ropery, Abel Chapman's, in the California Beck area dating from 1747.

Whitby Gasworks opened in the 1860s. Whitby was one of the first places in Britain to have gas lighting (the lamp that never goes out), benefitting as it did from the whale oil gas extracted from whale blubber from 1825. North Sea gas snuffed it out.

A milkman and a donkey.

John Stevenson or John the Bellman in Flowergate, the Whitby town crier. This proclamation was for a furniture auction in 1904.

A girl hard at work knitting socks or jumpers for the fishermen at the end of the West Pier. (A Frank Meadow Sutcliffe photograph)

A Christmas window at Brooksbanks game shop at No. 87 Church Street, c. 1910. (A Frank Meadow Sutcliffe photograph)

Whitby fishermen repairing crab pots by the harbour. John Thomas Ross took this around 1908.

In the jet works of William Wright in Haggersgate, apparently the only workshop equipped with gas engine-powered lathes.

Johnson's Yard.

New Way Ghaut.

Arguments Yard in 1895. As with many yards they were named after the family living within.

TOURISM

Whitby developed as a spa town in Georgian times when its three chalybeate springs were in demand for their medicinal and tonic qualities. Visitors flocked to the town leading to the building of lodging houses and hotels, mainly on the West Cliff. Things really took off, though, with the arrival of the railway in 1839 when the Whitby & Pickering Railway connecting Whitby to Pickering and eventually to the national hub that was York, and played a seminal part in the town's development as a tourism destination and as a trading port. Before the railways, access to the town was by laboriously slow by horse, cart and carriage. Trade was sluggish, and the town's fish only ever reached as far as York by packhorses staging from pub to pub en route.

In July 1844 the Pickering and Scarborough line was approved. In June 1845 the Whitby & Pickering Railway was bought by the YNMR, and the York to Pickering line opened in July 1845 affording a through route from York to Whitby. The mercurial George Hudson, who promoted the link to York, saw the incipient demand for accommodation from visitors from all over the country and was responsible for the construction of the Royal Crescent. His plans were to out-Bath Bath and its stunning crescent, but his reputation collapsed, as did his fortune, and only half of his ambitious plans were ever actually built.

Hudson's link to Whitby opened up the town as a popular destination for large numbers of factory workers from the West Riding and Teesside. Day trips and longer stay – overnight – trips became accessible and affordable. To facilitate construction of the required accommodation for the influx of visitors, Hudson had the Khyber Pass carved out of the West Cliff to transport the building materials, not least for the development of his Royal Crescent.

Whitby railway station serves the town. It is the terminus of the Esk Valley line from Middlesbrough, which is operated by Northern. It was formerly the northern terminus of the Whitby, Pickering and York line. In 2007 the North Yorkshire Moors Railway began a steam locomotive summer service between Pickering and Whitby as an extension of their long-standing and highly popular Pickering–Grosmont service. The Scarborough & Whitby Railway, built in 1885, followed a scenic route along the coast, taking in the thirteen-arch red-brick Larpool Viaduct across the Esk Valley into Whitby.

The line fell victim to Beeching in 1965, and the track bed is now used as a footpath, bridleway and by cyclists. The Whitby, Redcar & Middlesbrough Union Railway had a station at Whitby West Cliff from 1883 to 1958.

Whitby tourism in 2018.

Boat trips in Whitby.

The Promenade from West Cliff.

Above: Dracula Experience.

Left: The station doorway, 1895. This was taken by Frank Sutcliffe on 19 September 1895, showing Whitby Dock End. The vessel in view is the *Anna*.

The scene today with the *Endeavour* replica in the frame.

Posted in August in 1905, this Ross postcard brilliantly captures the age of the bathing machine. Most of them were owned by a local family firm by the name of Argument. When the customer was on board, they were drawn out into the deeper water. The bathers changed inside, having paid their 6*d* for a half hour's experience, and entered the water from the front steps. Men and women had separate sections of the beach for this activity in order to avoid too much excitement. Note the lovely Edwardian outfits – probably too overdressed for the sands by our way of modern thinking.

Above: The Royal Crescent.

Below: Larpool Viaduct, also known as the Esk Valley Viaduct.

Right: The men who built the viaduct with brickies brandishing tools of their trade. The hod carriers here brought every one of the million or so bricks from the ground to the top.

Below: A Frank Sutcliffe photograph showing the construction of the Whitby to Loftus line in the late 1870s, here at the mouth of the Grinkle tunnel.

The town attracted artists, and amateur and professional photographers, not least Frank Meadow Sutcliffe (1853–1941), whose work can be seen in the Sutcliffe Gallery in Flowergate. Sutcliffe lived in Broomfield Terrace with a business in Skinner Street in Whitby before moving to Sleights. His most famous photograph is *Water Rats*, which featured naked children playing in a boat. Even though the image is decidedly not erotic Sutcliffe was, however, excommunicated by his local clergy, as they thought it would 'corrupt' the opposite sex. Edward VII (then the Prince of Wales) later bought a copy.

The famous 199 steps have, over the years, challenged many an aging visitor and improved the arithmetic of many more children as they count their way up and down. The road to the right as you go up is the Donkey Road, which in 1370 was cut into the side where Lord Mulgrave drove his coach to visit Miss Anne Elizabeth Cholmley at Abbey House. He married her in 1787. When he was descending Donkey Road it was said that the hitched two horses to act as brakes on the steep descent.

Pannett Park houses the Whitby Museum and Art Gallery, which opened in 1931. The Chapman Wing (1954) is home to the Cook and Scoresby section and includes model ships and books on shipping. The museum was created by the Whitby Literary and Philosophical Society, which was founded in 1822. Visitor numbers in 1824 were 300, but today's yearly average is 40,000.

The Whitby Regatta takes place annually over three days in August. The competition between three rowing clubs – Whitby Friendship ARC, Whitby Fishermen's ARC and Scarborough ARC – is the highlight of the weekend. The event now includes a fair on the pier, demonstrations, fireworks and military displays – including a zoom past by the Red Arrows aerobatics display team of the Royal Air Force.

Tourism, then, is an increasingly important part of Whitby's economy with increasing numbers of people employed. The beautiful hinterland that is the North York Moors, the essentially British ambience of the seaside and a tangible fishing community with its quay and kippers, nearby deposits of fossils, the Gothic tradition, the abundance of jet jewellery, the heritage of Cook, Scoresby, whaling, press gangs and smugglers, the haunting beauty of the ruinous abbey and the still thriving St Mary's Church at the top of the 199 steps and the breathtaking views on the way up and at the top, all conspires to produce a magical festival of tourism.

Whitby children playing jacks, by Frank Sutcliffe. Jacks was a game played with a round stone or ball and five stones. You threw the ball into the air and had to pick up as many of the stones as possible with one hand before the ball hit the ground. The scene is at the foot of the 199 steps outside David Storry's grocery shop.

The steps today with St Mary's tower at the top.

The regatta in 1909.

The North York Moors National Park Authority Report on the economy of Whitby (2015) tells us how things were in Whitby. Sectors supporting the tourist trade such as accommodation, retail and food services employed 32 per cent of the total workforce in Whitby. That equates to 1,007 people, about one out of every thirteen Whitby residents.

Visit England reports that more British holidaymakers visit the North Yorkshire coast than any other part of the country outside London with the area receiving on average 1.4 million trips per year.

As with any seaside town, Whitby can boast a plethora of cafés, tearooms, pubs and fish and chip shops. Easily the best café is Sherlocks in Flowergate. The interior is exquisitely decorated over two floors with book-lined walls and artworks.

Gothic weekend goings-on.

Sherlocks.

Sherlocks Café.

Lobster baskets on the quay and the *Endeavour* replica.

The stunning *Endeavour* replica.

WHITBY AND THE ARTS

Given its small size and its relatively remote situation and distance from the cultural centres of Britain, Whitby has enjoyed a rich and resonant literary history. Indeed, the earliest English literature originates in Whitby with Caedmon, our first known Anglo-Saxon poet. There is also speculation that a nun from Whitby Abbey is the author of the Latin *Life of Pope Gregory I*, one of England's oldest texts (Andrew Breeze (2012), 'Did a Woman Write The Whitby Life of St Gregory?', *Northern History*, 49:2, p. 345–50).

Another scholarly article argues the case that women, including Hilda of Whitby and the author of the *Life of Pope Gregory,* were amongst the first women writers in English literature:

> This article argues that texts by women were 'overwritten' by the earliest male monastic writers, a process reinforced by later scholarship. By focusing on texts associated with religious houses ruled by women, and by seeing them as the productions not of individuals but of communities, it is possible to get a fuller and more balanced understanding of women's writing in this earliest period of English literary history. (Diane Watt (2013), 'The Earliest Women's Writing? Anglo-Saxon Literary Cultures and Communities', *Women's Writing*, 20:4, p. 537–54)

Things really got going in the mid-nineteenth century.

ELIZABETH GASKELL (1810–65)

She set a whole novel on the North Yorkshire coast [Sylvia's Lovers] and although she only visited Whitby briefly for a fortnight in 1859, she seems to have some hereditary affinity with the landscape, so powerfully does she evoke it.

Margaret Drabble, *A Writer's Britain: Landscape in Britain*.

Despite being born in the rarefied and relative luxury of a house in Chelsea's Lindsey Row (now No. 93 Cheyne Walk) Elizabeth Gaskell has a strong reputation for delineating northern industrial landscapes generally (not least in her *North and South*), and one Yorkshire landscape in particular – Whitby, where she sets *Sylvia's Lovers*. In 1832 Elizabeth married William Gaskell, the assistant minister at Cross Street Unitarian Chapel in Manchester, and moved with him to the city where the unremitting industrial surroundings started to exert an influence on Elizabeth's writing, informing her work in the industrial genre.

Sylvia's Lovers (1863) opens in the 1790s in the coastal town of Monkshaven, for which Whitby, then a thriving Greenland whaling port, is the model. Press gangs are rife during these early years of the Napoleonic Wars. Sylvia Robson is living with her parents on a farm, loved by her somewhat boring Quaker cousin Philip Hepburn. Sylvia, however, meets and falls in love with Charlie Kinraid, a far more exciting prospect who is a whaling speksioneer on a Whitby whaler, and they secretly get engaged. When Kinraid returns to his ship, he is, unfortunately, press-ganged away into the Royal Navy.

Gaskell's research for the book largely took the form of correspondence, not least with Dr William Scoresby, the famous Arctic explorer and former captain of a Whitby whaler. Scoresby was born in the village of Cropton, 26 miles south of Whitby. This research obviously focussed on the eighteenth century and, more specifically, press gangs, Whitby and whaling. However, in 1859 she visited the town for a fortnight with daughters Meta and Julia to see and experience the place for herself. A blue plaque commemorates her stay at No. 1 Abbey Terrace. Here is how Gaskell introduces her Whitby:

A great monastery [Whitby Abbey] had stood on those cliffs, overlooking the vast ocean that blended with the distant sky. Monkshaven itself was built by the side of the Dee, just where the river falls into the German Ocean. The principal street of the town ran parallel to the stream, and smaller lanes branched out of this, and straggled up the sides of the steep hill, between which and the river the houses were pent in. There was a bridge across the Dee, and consequently a Bridge Street running at right angles to the High Street; and on the south side of the stream there were a few houses of more pretension, around which lay gardens and fields. It was on this side of the town that the local aristocracy lived. And who were the great people of this small town? Not the younger branches of the county families that held hereditary state in their manor-houses on the wild bleak moors, that shut in Monkshaven almost as effectually on the land side as ever the waters did on the sea-board. No; these old families kept aloof from the unsavoury yet adventurous trade which brought wealth to generation after generation of certain families in Monkshaven.

The magnates of Monkshaven were those who had the largest number of ships engaged in the whaling-trade... Every one depended on the whale fishery, and almost every male inhabitant had been, or hoped to be, a sailor. Down by the river the smell was almost intolerable to any but Monkshaven people during certain seasons of the year; but on these unsavoury 'staithes' the old men and children lounged for hours, almost as if they revelled in the odours of train-oil.

MARGARET STORM JAMESON (1891-1986)

Storm Jameson was born in Whitby into a family that can trace its Whitby roots back some 600 years. Her father was a sea captain, and her mother was from an old established local family shipping firm.

Storm Jameson grew up at No. 5 Park Terrace, North Bank, before moving to West Cliff. She went to Scarborough Municipal School and won one of the three North Riding scholarships to Leeds University where she gained a first in English Literature and Language.

Whitby features extensively in her autobiography *Journey From the North* (1969). Volume one tells of her childhood in Whitby before the First World War, the strong relationship she enjoyed with her mother, her love of the sea and her academic achievements at university.

The view from the church door of St Mary's Church.

Much of her work is autobiographical, at least in part, and the landscapes and seascapes she saw all around her are clearly evident. Whitby gave her the model for Danesacre, a town which crops up in several of her books. It's there in *None Turn Back* and *The Road from the Monument*. Whitby (Danesacre) is Wik in *The Moon is Making*. Storm Jameson came back to Whitby frequently to visit her family, and also lived for a time at nearby Ruswarp. She wrote *A Day Off* (1933) in a moorland house near to Whitby in which she had lived since 1929.

The Triumph of Time trilogy (based on her own family history) – *The Lovely Ship* (1927), *The Voyage Home* (1930) and *A Richer Dust* (1931) – is full of descriptions of Whitby, while the Mary Hervey Russell books – *Company Parade* (1934), *The Mirror in Darkness I: Love in Winter* (1935), *The Mirror in Darkness II: None Turn Back* (1936) *The Mirror in Darkness III: The Journal of Mary Hervey Russell* (1945), *Before the Crossing* (1947) and *The Black Laurel* (1947) all tell the story of Mary Hansyke, later Mary Hervey, from her birth in 1841 to her death in 1923. Mary is based on the life of her own grandmother who came from a long line of shipbuilders and who took over the running of the business herself. In 1932 Storm Jameson, like Winifred Holtby, became close friends with Vera Brittain.

In *Company Parade* (1934) Storm Jameson describes how one of the characters, Russell Harvey, and her mother attend the 1921 Armistice Day service at St Mary's Church, and describes the view from the church door overlooking the harbour, the hills around it and the sea. The book ends with the main character looking down on Danesacre from the road above the town. She wants to love Danesacre but she can't – she wants to go back to London.

MARY LINSKILL (1840–91)

Novelist, short-story writer and poet Mary Linskill was born in Blackburn's Yard, off Church Street, in Whitby where her father was a jet worker and town constable. The landscape, the north seascape and the scenery of Yorkshire runs through much of her work. When her father died the family were left impoverished. Linskill, therefore, left school at the age of twelve and found work as an apprentice milliner in Charles Wilson's shop. She relocated to nearby Newholm-cum-Dunsley and later moved away from Whitby to Manchester and then Newcastle-under-Lyme, became a teacher in Nottingham and a governess in Derby. Writing was her aim and ambition, and eventually one of her serials was published in *Good Words*, a popular magazine of the day for which she became a regular contributor.

BLACKBURN'S YARD TODAY

In 1871 she published *Tales of the North Riding* (under the pseudonym Stephen York), which, as the title suggests, is redolent of Yorkshire, assuring her reputation as a writer. From 1871 she devoted herself to full-time writing, returning to Blackburn's Yard to be with her parents and pursue her writing career, but she found the noise of the many people in the cramped yard made composition difficult, except in the very early morning. She therefore stayed some time first at Staithes, a beautiful village 10 miles up the coast, and then at Ruswarp with a Mrs Taylor, but after a while poverty drove her back to Whitby in 1880.

Blackburn's Yard today.

It seems she also spent time at Newholme:

At this time she rented what was then called Wharnbeck Cottage in Newholm; it has since come to be known as Clevedon Cottage, after her first book. She stayed there for some years before returning to Whitby in 1880. At Newholm, as well as writing, [she] taught her maid (Emma Hodgson, whom she called Serena to distinguish her from her sister Emma) to read and write, formed a choir at the local church, and gave music lessons. Stamp says that the curate at Newholm, Tilden Smith, proposed to her at this time but was rejected. (www.orlando. cambridge.org/protected/svPeople?people_tab=3&formname=r&heading=h&person_ id=linsma#Whitby)

When she left Newholm, where she had survived virtual starvation and depression, she moved back with her mother, not to Blackburn's Yard but to a Georgian house at the end of a terrace in Spring Vale, now called Linskill Cottage. She later died here age fifty of a stroke.

The Haven under the Hill (1886) gives more of Whitby as well as a perceptive description of the Leeds Music Festival of 1883, which Dorigen, her hero, attends. It also gives a graphic picture of the jet-working industry – a major part of the local economy – and shines a light into the lives of the jet workers.

Rock slips were another feature of Whitby life and Linskill has no qualms about describing this macabre and disturbing incident:

During Dorigen's childhood … Salvain cautions Dorigen about the safety of the cliffs in the surrounding area: 'The cliff looks frightfully dangerous when you look up from below; indeed it is dangerous. You must never sit down under it, my dear. Once – it was in the year 1808 – two young Staithes girls, sisters they were, sat down on the scaur – I'll show you the exact spot when we go down – and while they were sitting there talking quietly together and looking out over the sea, a sharp splinter of rock fell from the top of the cliff, spinning round and round as it fell, and it struck one of the sisters on the back of the neck, so that it took her head quite off. The other sister saw it rolling away over the scaur to a great distance before it stopped. Think of that, my dear, whenever you are tempted to sit down under the cliffs. It is quite true, and what has happened once may always happen again.'

The story is corroborated in the *Saturday Magazine* for 27 July 1833.

In 1887, *Between the Heather and the Northern Sea* was published and illuminated yet more of nineteenth-century Whitby life. The book includes the story based on one of the most unusual sea rescues ever when in January 1881 the brig *Visitor* foundered off the bay during a blizzard. The lifeboat crew took to their boat, but were forced to remain outside the harbour.

Other works include the 1886 *Hagar: a North Yorkshire Pastoral*, which is all about Yorkshire coast and country folk; *In Exchange for a Soul: A Novel* (1887) tells how a Yorkshire fisher girl rises to be the wife of the squire.

Linskill died at Stakesby Vale, Whitby, and was initially buried in an unmarked grave. She was known as the 'Whitby Novelist' or as the 'novelist of the North' whose characters were 'portraits of Northern folk, as they who have lived among them will recognise, and her scenery is precisely what one recalls' (Jan Hewitt, 'The "Haven" and the "Grisly Rokkes": Mary Linskill's Dangerous Landscapes and the Making of Whitby' in *Northern Landscapes: Representations and Realities*, ed. T. Faulkner (Newcastle-upon-Tyne: 2010), p. 280).

BRAM STOKER (1847–1912)

The master of a particularly lurid and creepy kind of fiction,
represented by Dracula and other novels
'Death of Mr Bram Stoker', *The Times*, 22 April 1912

Abraham 'Bram' Stoker has provided us with one of the England's famous and haunting Yorkshire literary landscapes by making Whitby the setting for his famous Gothic novel *Dracula*, which was published in 1897. The associations live on to this day with the (not too) terrifying 'Dracula Experience', (un)spooky Dracula walks with commentary, a Bram Stoker Film Festival, productions of *Dracula* in the abbey ruins, and an annual goth weekend which fills the town with wonderful goth costumes, goth make-up, goth music and, of course, unfettered Gothic fear. All of this is comparatively easy to achieve due to the unique ambience and aura of Whitby – an atmosphere that would have shrouded Stoker on his morning walks and that persists to this day.

The chapters set in Whitby (six to eight) are the product of Stoker's impressive knowledge and affection for the charming seaport which he first visited in 1885, followed by other visits until 1890. Staying at Mrs Veazey's guesthouse at 6 Royal Crescent, he also took in the delightful harbours of Ravenscar and Robin Hood's Bay fourteen miles and five miles south of Whitby respectively.

By 1885 Whitby had a reputation as a very pleasant seaside town and as something of a writers' colony, playing host to the likes of Charles Dickens, Wilkie Collins and Henry James – all looking for land – and seascape inspiration. Whitby has both in spades, whichever way you look and wherever you are.

For the name of his creation, Count Dracula, look no further than in a book he was browsing in Whitby library, then at the Coffee House End of the Quay. The book was William Wilkinson's *An Account of the Principalities of Wallachia and Moldavia* published in 1820 (Wilkinson had been British consul in Bucharest). Significantly Wilkinson referred to a fifteenth-century prince called Vlad Tepes who was in the habit of impaling his enemies on wooden stakes. He was called Dracula – the 'son of the dragon'. A footnote further informed Stoker that

Dracula in the Wallachian language means Devil. The Wallachians at that time … used to give this as a surname to any person who rendered himself conspicuous either by courage, cruel actions, or cunning.

Stoker would have heard of the shipwreck five years earlier of a Russian vessel called the *Dmitry*, from Narva. This ran aground on Tate Hill Sands below East Cliff, carrying a cargo of silver sand. These names fall easily into the *Demeter* from Varna, the Russian schooner en route to London that carried Dracula to Whitby laden with a cargo of silver sand and boxes of Transylvanian earth. She ran aground on Tate Hill Sands, crew missing, its dead skipper lashed to the wheel. This is how Stoker describes the *Demeter* making landfall at Whitby with Dracula, in the guise of a huge hound, bounding ashore:

But, strangest of all, the very instant the shore was touched, an immense dog sprang up on deck from below … and running forward, jumped from the bow on to the sand. Making straight for the steep cliff, where the churchyard hangs over the laneway to the East Pier … it disappeared in the darkness.

Vlad Țepeș, the Impaler, Prince of Wallachia (1456–62) (d. 1477). (Kunsthistorisches Museum Wien, Gemäldegalerie Ambras castle bei Innsbruck. Photographer www. neuramagazine.com/dracula-triennale-di-milano/image)

The 199 Steps.

Whitby Pier.

The graveyard.

The ghostly abbey ruins as Stoker, and Dracula, would have seen them.

This sets the scene nicely for what was to come.

That steep cliff, and its 199 steps, the Church Stairs, which gradually reveal more and more of the attractive red pantiled town below, lead to what must be one of the most atmospheric graveyards in the land – even on a sunny, blue-sky day the consecrated space around St Mary's looks, and feels, foggy. Add to that the wrecked majesty of the abbey, which looms above the church, and its serried ranks of crooked tombs standing sentinel high above the thrashing sea and you have the perfect landscape in which to set a horror story of uncanny and eerily tangible atmosphere. Here it was that Lucy Westenra was attacked by the count. Mina Murray – whose experiences are central to the novel – records in her diary:

> Right over the town is the ruin of Whitby Abbey, which was sacked by the Danes, and which is the scene of part of 'Marmion,' where the girl was built up in the wall. It is a most noble ruin, of immense size, and full of beautiful and romantic bits; there is a legend that a white lady is seen in one of the windows.

Stoker plundered the inscriptions on the church gravestones for names to use in the book – literally literary grave robbing.

JOHN RONALD REUEL TOLKIEN (1892–1973)

Tolkien went to Whitby twice, in 1910 and 1945, imbibing the extensive Anglo-Saxon history to be found there. This particular Yorkshire landscape and the lost villages in the vicinity like Ravenser Odd may well have made a contribution to his many *Lord of the Rings* references to the ruin and decay of a once flourishing civilisation.

BARBARA HEPWORTH (1903–75)

Hepworth was born in Wakefield into an upwardly mobile family, and her father encouraged her to get on in life. Significantly, as a child she accompanied her father, Herbert, when he travelled all over the West Yorkshire countryside with his job as a civil engineer for the West Riding County Council, and, from 1921, county surveyor. Hepworth attended Wakefield Girls' High School and won a music scholarship in 1915 and an open scholarship in 1917. Summer holidays, significantly again, were spent at beautiful Robin Hood's Bay. These were not the usual bucket and spade and donkey ride affairs. Hepworth's beach holidays were not without influence and came back to delight her later in life:

> My father took us each year to Robin Hood's Bay to stay in a house on the lovely beach … here I laid out my paints and general paraphernalia and crept out at dawn to collect stones, seaweeds and paint, and draw by myself before somebody organised me!
>
> From *Barbara Hepworth, A Pictorial Autobiography* (Bath: 1971)

A. S. BYATT (B. 1936)

In 1990 Byatt published *Possession: A Romance* in which the exigencies of their research project lead academics Roland and Maud to Yorkshire in their pursuit of the Victorian poets Randolph Ash and Christabel LaMotte. Attracted by the place name Boggle Hole ('a nice word') Roland suggests a detour. Over 100 years before, Randolph Ash and Christabel LaMotte were themselves on the Yorkshire coast in 1860:

'He [Ash] remembered most, when it was over, when time had run out, the day they had spent in a place called Boggle Hole, where they had gone because they liked the word.'

The reference to Boggle Hole must surely have been inspired by Byatt's memories of seaside family holidays in Filey as a young girl. Boggle Hole is a pretty inlet south of Robin Hood's Bay. A boggle is a local name for a hobgoblin, the 'little people' who lived in caves along this coast and in the more remote corners of the North York Moors. More prosaically Boggle Hole itself was where smugglers used to land their prodigious contraband.

Roland and Maud come to the conclusion that LaMotte's poem 'Melusina' has got to be set in Yorkshire — 'it's full of local words from here, gills and riggs and ling ... she talks about the air like summer colts playing on the moor. That's a Yorkshire saying.' Arriving at Thomason Foss, the academics realise that this was part of the specific setting for *Melusina*. Byatt is using a literary landscape of her own to illuminate the very same literary landscape deployed by Christabel LaMotte. This walk around Goathland and Mallyan Spout recreates a similar treck described by Ash in a letter at the beginning of chapter 14 in which he mentions 'Eller Beck' and the wonderful, valley-deep 'Beck Holes'.

Lewis Carroll stayed at 5, East Terrace between July and September 1854. Charles Dickens visited Whitby, mentioning the town in a letter of 1861 to his friend Wilkie Collins, who was at the time staying in Whitby:

Boggle Hole Youth Hostel in the 1950s.

In my time that curious railroad by the Whitby Moor was so much the more curious, that you were balanced against a counter-weight of water, and that you did it like Blondin. But in these remote days the one inn of Whitby was up a back-yard, and oyster-shell grottoes were the only view from the best private room.

Collins stayed in Whitby to work on his novel, *No Name*, accompanied by Caroline Graves, the inspiration for *The Woman in White*.

James Russell Lowell visited Whitby while ambassador in London 1880–85, staying at No. 3 Wellington Terrace, West Cliff. On his last visit in 1889, he wrote:

'This is my ninth year at Whitby and the place loses none of its charm for me'.

Henry James and George du Maurier apparently visited too:

[David] Lodge says [in *Author, Author*] James visited Whitby in 1887, when both the du Maurier family and Lowell were there; in 1889, 'when Lowell alone was the attraction'; and in 1893, when 'he took Lowell's old rooms in a cottage down by the harbour, near the drawbridge', and one morning walked to Staithes with du Maurier. James certainly made visits to Lowell at Whitby in 1887 and 1889, and stayed in Lowell's old rooms in 1893; but the rooms were with the Misses Gallilee at 3 Wellington Terrace, not a cottage by the harbour…

The Pavilion Theatre built in the 1870s at West Cliff hosts a range of events during the summer months. For over four decades the town has hosted the Whitby Folk Week; 2019 sees over 300 concerts over seven days spread across fifty venues with over 100 artists ready to entertain. Whitby Blues, Rhythm & Rock Festival is in October.

Since 1993 the bi-annual (April and October) Whitby Goth Weekend for adherents to Goth subculture attracts avid Goths from all over the world. Since 2008, the Bram Stoker Film Festival has taken place in October.

The Folk Festival in 2015.

The Bram Stoker Film Festival.

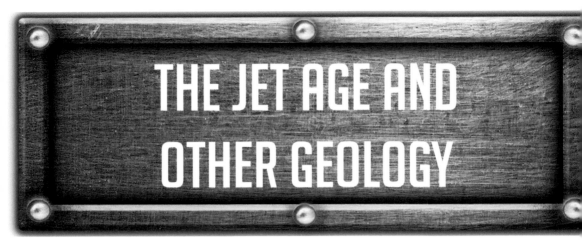

THE JET AGE AND OTHER GEOLOGY

The website www.genuki.org.uk/big/eng/YKS/NRY/Whitby/WhitbyHistory has by far the best account of Whitby's geological treasures:

> The neighbourhood of Whitby abounds with natural curiosities; and the various petrifactions almost every where found in the alum rocks have long excited wonder and puzzled philosophy. Besides the petrified shells of sea-fish, others have been found in the scarr or cliff on the east side of the mouth of the Eske, which cannot be arranged under any class. In the early part of the last century Dr. Woodward, dug up on the scarr the petrified arm and hand of a man in which all the bones and joints were perfectly visible. In 1743, the Rev. Mr. Borwick found in the alum-rock the complete skeleton or petrified bones of a man, and sent it, though in a mutilated state to one of our Universities to enrich their museum. After this, in the year 1758, the petrified bones of a crocodile, an animal never known in this part of the world was taken out of the rock and sent to the Royal Society, in whose transactions at in Vol. L. Part II. It is described; and about four years after the skeleton of a petrified horse was found in the alum works at Saltwick, at the depth of thirty yards under ground, and sent as a natural rarity to the University of Aberdeen (Charlton's *History of Whitby*).
>
> The ammonitae or snake stones, as already mentioned, are found in almost every place where the alum rock exists, and particularly in Whitby Scarr, between high and low water mark. The snakes are all inclosed in hard elliptical stones, which seem to have been struck within, being coiled up in spiral volutes, and every way resembling that reptile in their form and shape, save only in the head, which is always wanting. There are two different species: the round bodied and the flat bodied. The round bodied are girt or encompassed from end to end with semicircular channels or cavities, while the other have a ridge on their back, and are plated on the sides, as if they had been pressed together, the marks wherewith they are pitted, resembling the impression of a man's thumb on a soft substance. The snakes are all enclosed in hard elliptical stones, which seems to be of a different mineral from the snake itself, which may, by care, be separated from it. These ammonitae are noticed by Camden and Leland, and both of them observe, that fame ascribes them to the power of St Hilda's prayers. This is of course a superstition that is much easier to reject than it is satisfactorily to account for the phenomenon.

Above and below: Natural Wonders in Grape Lane, the place to go for fossils.

Whitby Scaur.

HOME OF LIAS AND ZOOLITES

During the First World War, the steel shortage led to the construction of a number of experimental ships made from reinforced concrete. In 1927 the *Creteblock* was decommissioned and the hulk languished in Whitby harbour until after the Second World War, when it was towed out to sea to be sunk. On 22 August 1948 *Creteblock* was finally towed out, but instead of ending up at the bottom of the sea it sank on the Scaur, where she remains to this day.

GEORGE YOUNG

George Young was born in 1777 on small farm near Edinburgh. Had he not been born with only one hand he would probably have graduated into a farming life rather than the successful academic career he pursued at the University of Edinburgh. In 1801, he arrived in Whitby as pastor to the United Associate or new Presbyterian Congregation chapel in Cliff Street. Young was able to divide his time between his ministry and his passion for geology and palaeontology in Whitby's productive landscape.

Young married Margaret Hunter, a Whitby girl, achieving fame with the publication of his *A History of Whitby and Streonsalh Abbey* in 1817. He followed this with 'A Geological Survey of the Yorkshire Coast, describing the strata and fossils between the Humber and the Tees from the German Ocean to the Plain of York.'

Young's greatest legacy was the Whitby Literary and Philosophical Society founded in 1823 by a group of Whitby people under his aegis. As the umbrella organisation for the Whitby Museum, it remains an active and vibrant part of the historic life of the town. The society's mission was to set up a museum specialising in fossils since 'Whitby is … abounding with petrifactions and containing not a few antiquities.' It duly opened in rooms over a shop in Baxtergate but soon moved to a building on the Quayside where it continued to grow.

Controversially, Young concluded, from his geological and theological studies, that 'there was good evidence for Noah's flood and further came to the opinion that God had created the world in six days around 6,000 years ago.' It gives us no small pleasure to observe that the geological facts which have come under our review do not contradict but confirm the sacred scriptures.

JET

It is the black mineraloid jet, the compressed remains (fossilised wood) of ancestors of the monkey puzzle tree (Araucariaceae), found in abundance in the cliffs and on the moors and used since the Bronze Age to make beads, which enjoys the greatest celebrity in Whitby and has done since Roman times, when hairpins and brooches were made of this, reaching its zenith during the reign of Victoria after the death of Prince Albert. The jet found around Whitby is of early Jurassic (Toarcian) period, approximately 182 million years old. The hardest, purest, saltwater jet comes from a 7.5-mile stretch of coast around Whitby, which yields some of the best deposits the earth has to offer. Whitby jet is light in weight, making it perfect for jewellery. It has a hardness of 3.5–4 on the Mohs hardness scale.

The jet industry declined dramatically from 1870 when prodigious quantities of inferior and cheaper Spanish jet was imported, critically injuring Whitby's production. Nevertheless, a number of shops still sell jet jewellery, mainly as souvenirs to tourists.

It is commonly believed that Albert's death in 1861 was the catalyst for the popularity and fashionable nature of jet. However, the first jet shop opened in Whitby in 1808 and there were fifty trading in 1850, which suggests that jet's appeal was already well established by the time Albert died. Victorian tourists couldn't get enough of the gleaming, black gold transmogrified into brooches, earrings and lockets. Around 1,400 Whitby people worked as jet finders, carvers or polishers – a massive one third of the town's population! But, even at the height of the market for jet jewellery the miners' wages were desperately low at approximately £1.25 per week for a six-day week.

The Whitby Jet Heritage Centre website tells how in 1851 a rare draft lease allows the miner 'to make all necessary drift tunnels and other works as shall be found necessary' for searching for, getting and removing the jet. This draft lease related to the cliffs near Gnipe Howe Farm, north-east of High Hawsker. It goes on to describe the dangers involved:

Much of the mining along the cliff face was done by lowering the miners over the edge of the cliff face on makeshift rope harnesses. Inland mining was done by digging tunnels 'drifts' into the soft hillside with picks until the shale became too hard to mine. Once a drift had been exhausted the miners would dig a new drift until they had created a warren of tunnels. Large stone pillars were used to support the tunnels however the miners were faced with the ever present danger of the drifts collapsing. The waste shale from mining was deposited in spoil heaps which we can still see the evidence of today on the hills around Rosedale and Bilsdale. (https://www.whitbyjet.co.uk/about-jet-read-more)

The 1901 Wesley Hall, which has been tastefully converted into the Museum of Whitby Jet.

The old workshop in the Whitby Jet Heritage Centre.

The world's only surviving Victorian jet workshop is in Whitby, at the Whitby Jet Heritage Centre in Church Street. The website describes this fascinating piece of the town's history:

This genuine Victorian jet workshop was discovered by chance in the attic of a derelict property in Burns Yard, Whitby. A local builder had purchased the property and during the course of renovation work he knocked a wall down, discovering the workshop which has been completely sealed in the building. We feel privileged to be the custodians of this unique and historic piece of Whitby's Heritage. The workshop was carefully removed and set up at our premises shortly after its discovery so that many people may view the only remaining example of a Victorian jet workshop…The workshop was first registered in 1867 in White's industrial directory of North Yorkshire. It was one of approximately two hundred similar workshops employing fourteen hundred men…when the population of Whitby was just in excess of four thousand, meaning the industry employed a third of the population. With employment figures so high it was obviously a huge industry for Victorian Whitby and with an equivalent turnover of over three million pounds today it was also a major economic force It would have produced a variety of ornately carved jewellery and decorative items. (www.whitbyjet.co.uk/victorian-workshop)

See their website for some fascinating detail on the production process: from the foreman's bench to the pig bristle brush, taking in the grindstone, the rouge wheel and the walrus hide wheel along the way. According to Hal Redvers-Jones: 'Grinding was one of the dangerous jobs. The lad would put water on the stone all the time and sometimes it would weaken and fly into pieces; 900 revolutions per minute, straight into his chest. A few got killed that way.'

One of today's workshops.

The various stages in the production process depicted above the door.

THE FUTURE: POTASH AND WIND

Despite its rich heritage, it is clear that Whitby is by no means stuck in the past, dependent, like some other seaside resorts and small coastal ports, on fossilising industries with an ever-diminishing workforce. On the contrary, the town is perfectly placed to take advantage of new work opportunities, one of them afforded by emergent clean renewable energy industries. Whitby people will benefit from the work opportunities offered by both schemes.

Woodsmith Mine is a £2 billion deep polyhalite mine planned near Sneatonthorpe, Whitby. The project will mine the world's largest deposit of polyhalite. Polyhalite, a unique type of potash, is a naturally occurring fertilizer containing potassium, sulphur, magnesium and calcium – four of the six key nutrients that all plants need to grow. It can help farmers to increase productivity and can lead to better, more balanced fertilizer practices. When complete, it would be among the largest mining projects ever built in the United Kingdom. The project area will yield the largest highest grade resource of polyhalite to be found anywhere in the world. The polyhalite resource here comprises 2.66 billion tonnes. A recent report by independent analysts Quod found the project will deliver decades of major economic benefits for the UK and have a transformative impact on the local economy.

At full production the project will add £2.3 billion a year to UK GDP; create over 1,000 long-term, high-skilled, high-paid jobs; generate exports of £2.5 billion a year, reducing the UK's trade deficit by 7 per cent; and make annual tax contributions worth £472 million a year to pay for vital public services. The project is expected to permanently add up to 17 per cent to the economic output of North Yorkshire.

Despite the prospect of thousands of local jobs, many objections have been raised to the mine and the proposed conveyor that would transport the raw material offsite to Redcar and Teesport 23 miles away. However, some local people do support the venture. The farmer who works the land next to the mine site wrote to the NPA in support of the project saying, 'Please approve the application and stop the deteriorating living standards of the Whitby people. Stop the young moving out and plan to keep families together.' Another local man stated that there was nothing in the area other than pot washing or working in the local fish and chip restaurant.

The mine will produce 20 million tonnes a year of polyhalite, potash and POLY4 and is expected to be operational for 100 years. In August 2017, the 4,900-feet-deep tunnels were being constructed on the site.

Digging works at Woodsmith Mine.

Briony Fox, Director of Polyhalite Projects at the North York Moors National Park Authority, said:

'It's great to see work starting on the tunnel. There couldn't be a better solution to transport large amounts of polyhalite from the mine site to Wilton (Redcar) without having an impact on local roads and people's enjoyment of the National Park.

Whitby is the closest port to the proposed development of the Dogger Bank Wind Farm and is well placed to provide support vessel operations and logistics. The Dogger Bank development will consist of four offshore wind farms, each with a capacity of up to 1.2 gigawatts. Planning permission for the first phase of the project (Dogger Bank Creyke Beck) was granted by the UK government in February 2015, and consent for the second phase (Dogger Bank Teesside) was granted in August 2015. The Dogger Bank zone is located off the east Yorkshire coast 134 kilometres offshore and less than three hours steaming from Whitby (at 25 knots). It extends over an area approximately equivalent in size to North Yorkshire. It is a good location for offshore wind farms because it is well out of sight of land, far away from shore, avoiding complaints about the visual impact of wind turbines.

ABOUT THE AUTHOR

Paul Chrystal has worked in medical publishing for far too long but now combines this with writing features for national newspapers and history magazines, as well as appearing regularly on BBC local radio, on the BBC World Service and Radio 4's PM programme. Paul has also contributed to a forthcoming six-part series for BBC2 'celebrating the history of some of Britain's most iconic craft industries', in this case chocolate in York. He has been a history advisor for a number of York tourist attractions and is the author of 100 or so books on a wide range of subjects. Paul lives in Haxby, near York. From 2019 he will take over the editorship of *York Historian*, the journal of the Yorkshire Architectural and York Archaeological Society. In 2019 he is also guest speaker for the prestigious Vassar College New York's London Programme with Goldsmith University.

By the same author:
Bradford at Work
Doncaster at Work (in press)
Yorkshire Literary Landscapes
Pubs in & Around York
The North York Moors Through Time
Old Middlesbrough
Secret Middlesbrough
Lifeboat Stations of the North East
The Romans in the North of England [in press]
Redcar, Marske and Saltburn Through Time
Old Coatham & Redcar
The Place Names of Yorkshire
Yorkshire Murders, Manslaughter, Madness & Executions